Crossword Puzzle

Across

2 noun - tampon used to absorb menstrual flow

4 noun - a colorless flammable volatile liquid hydrocarbon used as a solvent

6 verb - make (assets) available; "release the holdings in the dictator's bank account"

8 verb - bend out of shape as under pressure or from heat; "The highway buckled during the heat wave"

9 Ancient European people

10 noun - a city in Uganda on the north shore of Lake Victoria

11 the arch of bone beneath the eye that forms the prominence of the cheek

Down

1 verb - form into a ball by winding or rolling; "ball wool"

3 adjective - surprisingly and unceremoniously brusque in manner; "an abrupt reply"

5 To walk or march across country

7 noun - the 19th letter of the Hebrew alphabet

9 verb - place a bet on; "Which horse are you backing?"; "I'm betting on the new horse"

Crossword Puzzle

Across

1 A boatman; an oarsman.

6 noun - Hindu god of wisdom or prophecy; the god who removes obstacles

8 adjective - brief and to the point; effectively cut short;

11 noun - Circassian people living east of the Black Sea

12 noun - goat-like antelope of central Eurasia having a stubby nose like a proboscis

Down

2 Appearance or image; a phantasm; a spectral image; also a mental image or idea.

3 small three-masted Mediterranean sailing ships with lateen and square sails

4 noun - a stiff hat made of straw with a flat crown

5 noun - an attribute of mischievous children

7 A stuffed jacket worn under the mail or (later) a jacket plated with mail.

9 a coffee cake flavored with orange rind and raisins and almonds

10 verb - feel intense anger; "Rage against the dying of the light!"

Crossword Puzzle

Across

2 (Yiddish) a thief or dishonest person or scoundrel (often used as a general term of abuse)

4 Skywalker of star wars

6 One who or that which warps or twists out of shape.

8 adverb - in a naive manner; "he believed naively that she would leave him her money"

11 noun - the agent to whom property involved in a bailment is delivered

Down

1 noun - Russian country house

3 verb - fill with high spirits; fill with optimism; "Music can uplift your spirits"

5 noun - a grey volcanic rock containing plagioclase and quartz and other crystalline minerals

7 noun - one of the inherent cognitive or perceptual powers of the mind

9 largest city and de facto capital of Nauru on the south-west coast

10 A small gable or gable-shaped canopy formed over a tabernacle niche etc.

Crossword Puzzle

Across

2 adjective - having freedom to move about; "vagile aquatic animals"

5 noun - gasoline jelled with aluminum soaps; highly incendiary liquid used in fire bombs and flamethrowers

7 noun - a car that has a long body and rear door with space behind rear seat

9 noun - (Greek mythology) a nymph of lakes and springs and rivers and fountains

11 verb - fall away or decline; "The patient's strength ebbed away"

12 Fitness regime that incorporates dance and martial arts movements

Down

1 A genus of small insectivores including the common European mole.

3 adjective - graceful and pleasing; "gainly conduct"; "a gainly youth with dark hair and eyes"

4 verb - make unhappy; "The news of her death saddened me"

6 noun - the basic unit of money in Western Samoa

8 adjective - lacking vitality as from weariness or illness or unhappiness; "a wan smile"

10 Secret; lonely; solitary; dreadful.

Crossword Puzzle

Across

2 Plaster as used in Persian architecture and decorative art.

4 noun - someone who assesses the monetary worth of possessions

7 A fee or toll paid for goods sold in a hall.

8 bedding made of two layers of cloth filled with stuffing and stitched together

10 noun - a Dardic language spoken by the Kafir in northeastern Afghanistan

11 small terrestrial viper common in northern Eurasia

Down

1 noun - the language of nomadic Lapps in northern Scandinavia and the Kola Peninsula

3 noun - a reckless impetuous irresponsible person

5 noun - the Siouan language spoken by the Dakota

6 noun - someone concerned with the science or art or business of cultivating the soil

8 noun - a wad of something chewable as tobacco

9 verb - increase (one's body weight); "She gained 20 pounds when she stopped exercising"

Crossword Puzzle

Across

2 noun - a city in southeastern Wisconsin on Lake Michigan to the south of Milwaukee

3 Given name from the prophet who advised King David in the Bible.

7 A twelfth part as of the Roman as; an ounce.

8 noun - a Dravidian language spoken in southern India

9 noun - periodic shedding of the cuticle in arthropods or the outer skin in reptiles

10 A worm which has its tail conspicuously colored.

12 the iridescent internal layer of a mollusk shell

Down

1 noun - an eight-sided polygon

4 noun - a transmitter used to broadcast electronic jamming

5 One who does anything good or bad; a doer; an agent.

6 noun - (Yiddish) glazed yeast-raised doughnut-shaped roll with hard crust

11 a genus of Platalea

Crossword Puzzle

Across

2 Industrial city of NE India capital of the state of Jharkand

5 verb - cook or heat in a microwave oven; "You can microwave the leftovers"

8 Abashed; confounded; discomfited.

10 verb - cause to be embarrassed; cause to feel self-conscious

11 A ditch on the outside of the counterscarp usually full of water.

12 adjective - having a quality that thrusts itself into attention;

Down

1 a south Indian soup flavoured with tamarind juice and spices

3 verb - emit a loud unpleasant kind of laughing

4 noun - the language of the Quechua which was spoken by the Incas

6 noun - the first dynasty of Arab caliphs whose capital was Damascus

7 verb - select from a list; "empanel prospective jurors"

9 noun - United States playwright who collaborated with many other writers including Moss Hart (1889-1961)

Crossword Puzzle

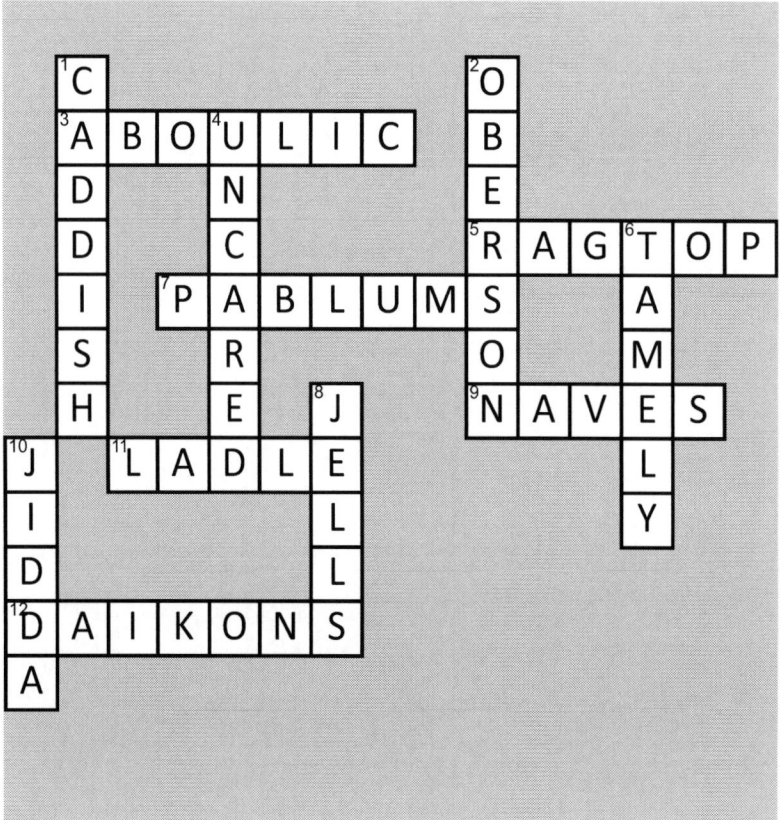

Across

3 adjective - suffering from abulia; showing abnormal inability to act or make decisions

5 slang for convertible top on a vehicle

7 noun - worthless or oversimplified ideas

9 the central area of a church

11 verb - remove with or as if with a ladle; "ladle the water out of the bowl"

12 noun - radish of Japan with a long hard durable root eaten raw or cooked

Down

1 adjective - offensively discourteous

2 noun - (Middle Ages) the king of the fairies and husband of Titania in medieval folklore

4 Not cared for; not heeded; -- with for.

6 adverb - in a tame manner; "the labour movement allowed itself to be run out of power tamely"

8 verb - become gelatinous; "the liquid jelled after we added the enzyme"

10 noun - port city in western Saudi Arabia on the Red Sea; near Mecca

Crossword Puzzle

Across

3 noun - a pastry cup with a filling of fruit or custard and no top crust

4 noun - a book in the Old Testament that tells the story of Jonah and the whale

9 Of or pertaining to a layman or the laity.

10 A long-tailed monkey of Borneo (Semnopithecus rubicundus). It has a tuft of long hair on the head.

12 noun - an Australian sheepdog with pointed ears

Down

1 verb - contact as with a pager or by calling somebody's name over a P.A. system

2 noun - a sad Portuguese folksong

5 An exclamation expressive of sorrow.

6 adjective - of a leaf shape; having leaflets or lobes radiating from a common point

7 noun - disparaging terms for the common people

8 To seal; to confirm as by a seal or stamp.

11 adjective - being eight more than forty

Crossword Puzzle

Across

2 make a noise characteristic of a goose; "Cackling geese"

6 noun - a metallic sound; "the jingle of coins"; "the jangle of spurs"

7 noun - a division of a prison (usually consisting of several cells)

9 A red crystalline dyestuff obtained by heating together pyrogallic and phthalic acids.

10 noun - a square piece of cloth used for wiping the eyes or nose or as a costume accessory

11 adjective - of or relating to or characteristic of the Sabines

Down

1 noun - loose long overcoat of heavy fabric; usually belted

3 noun - port city in western Saudi Arabia on the Red Sea; near Mecca

4 noun - a person who exercises control over workers;

5 noun - a refractive surgery procedure that reshapes the cornea

8 noun - a person who makes deceitful pretenses

Crossword Puzzle

Across

1. An old Italian silver coin worth about ten cents.
3. verb - permeate or impregnate; "The war drenched the country in blood"
6. noun - a filamentous projection or process on an organism
8. noun - a device for lighting or igniting fuel or charges or fires; "do you have a light?"
10. verb - contaminate with a disease or microorganism
12. noun - city in northwestern Jordan

Down

2. discrimination against middle-aged and elderly people
4. To remove the bung from; as to unbung a cask.
5. A cow house dairy house or cow pasture.
7. verb - terminate a pregnancy by undergoing an abortion
9. noun - a horse trained to a special gait in which both feet on one side leave the ground together
11. a city in west central Tunisia

Crossword Puzzle

Across

2 Hot; burning; ardent.

7 A kind of small turnip a variety of Brassica campestris. See Brassica.

8 noun - any of several fleet black-and-white striped African equines

9 verb - check the emission of (sound)

11 noun - the 4th letter of the Hebrew alphabet

12 verb - move with abrupt seemingly uncontrolled motions; "The patient's legs were jerkings"

Down

1 adjective - of someone who has not been married; "unwed mother"

3 adjective - liable to change; "an emotionally labile person"

4 verb - give in as to influence or pressure

5 verb - divide by two; divide into halves; "Halve the cake"

6 Former kingdom of the Basques.

10 noun - a machine for putting objects or substances into bags

Crossword Puzzle

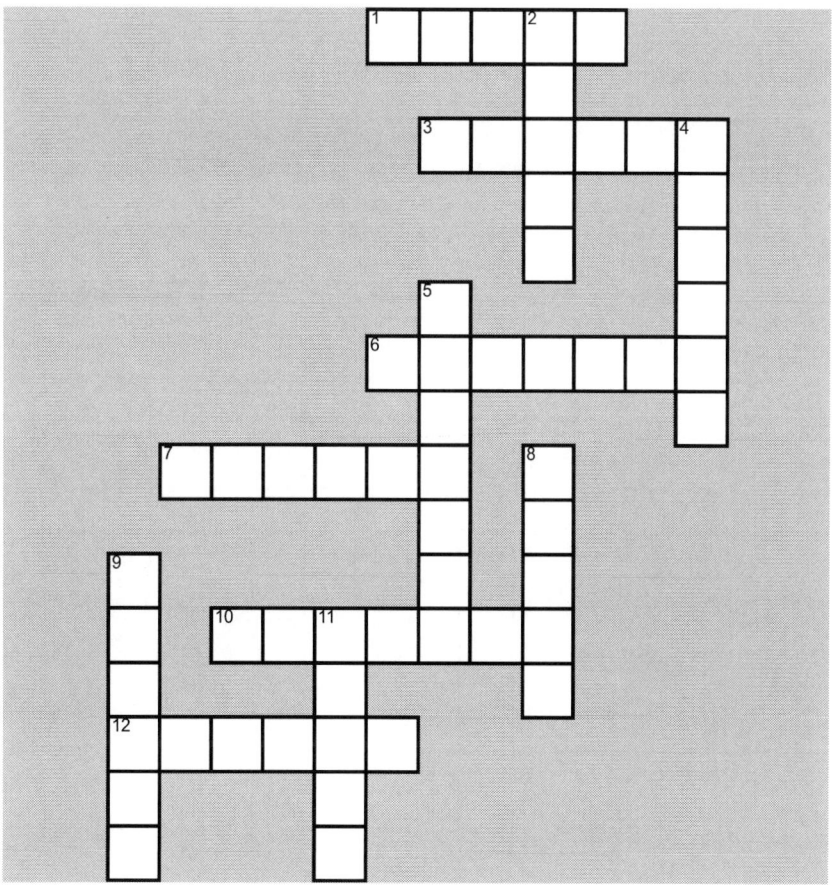

Across

1 verb - secrete or form water as tears or saliva;

3 noun - a soft-finned fish of the family Gadidae

6 verb - make moist; "The dew moistened the meadows"

7 verb - make a cackling sound; "The fire cackled cozily"

10 noun - the basic unit of money in Gambia

12 adjective - not yet brought into existence; "unborn generations"

Down

2 Relating to the Eddas; resembling the Eddas.

4 noun - a fabric of linen or cotton or silk or wool with a reversible pattern woven into it

5 noun - someone who guards prisoners

8 noun - offensive term for an openly homosexual man

9 a large island off the north east coast of Java

11 adjective - ostentatiously lofty in style; "a man given to large talk"; "tumid political prose"

Crossword Puzzle

Across

2 One of the 26 states of Brazil

4 noun - large mostly white Australian stork

5 noun - the second month of the Hindu calendar

8 verb - relieve oneself of troubling information

10 tropical west african tree with dark mahogany-like wood

Down

1 noun - a building containing public baths

3 attack with gas; subject to gas fumes; "The despot gassed the rebellious tribes"

6 adjective - having a mental age of three to seven years

7 Containing the remains of organized bodies; -- said of rock or soil.

8 To release from cords; to loosen the cord or cords of; to unfasten or unbind; as to uncord a package.

9 noun - cosmetics applied to the face to improve or change your appearance

Crossword Puzzle

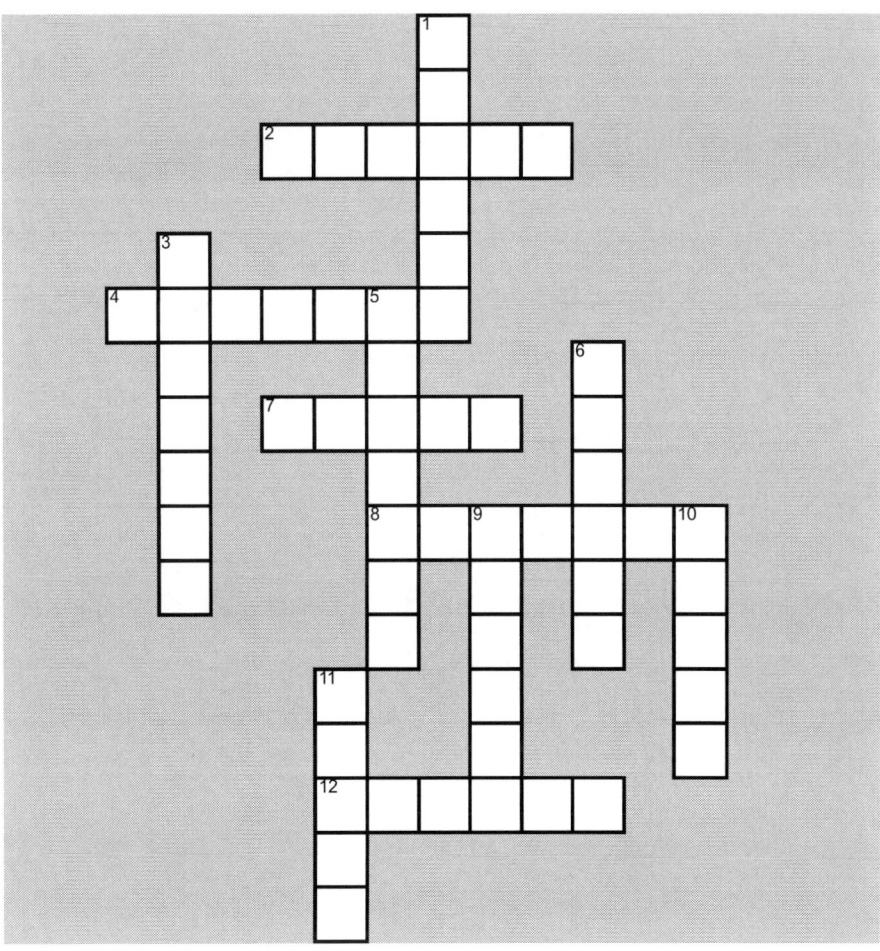

Across

2 noun - naturally occurring crystalline sodium chloride

4 verb - bob forward and under so as to feed off the bottom of a body of water; "dabbling ducks"

7 former president of uganda

8 set afire; "the ignited paper"; "a kindled fire"

12 verb - lessen pain or discomfort; alleviate; "ease the pain in your legs"

Down

1 noun - any of several tropical American trees some yielding economically important timber

3 noun - (Old Testament) son of Noah

5 verb - stain black to make it look like ebony

6 An instrument for scraping bones.

9 noun - shrub bearing oval-fruited kumquats

10 noun - god of agriculture and earth; counterpart of Phoenician Dagon

11 A word occurring in a corrupt passage of Bacon's Essays and probably meaning to stir to move.

Crossword Puzzle

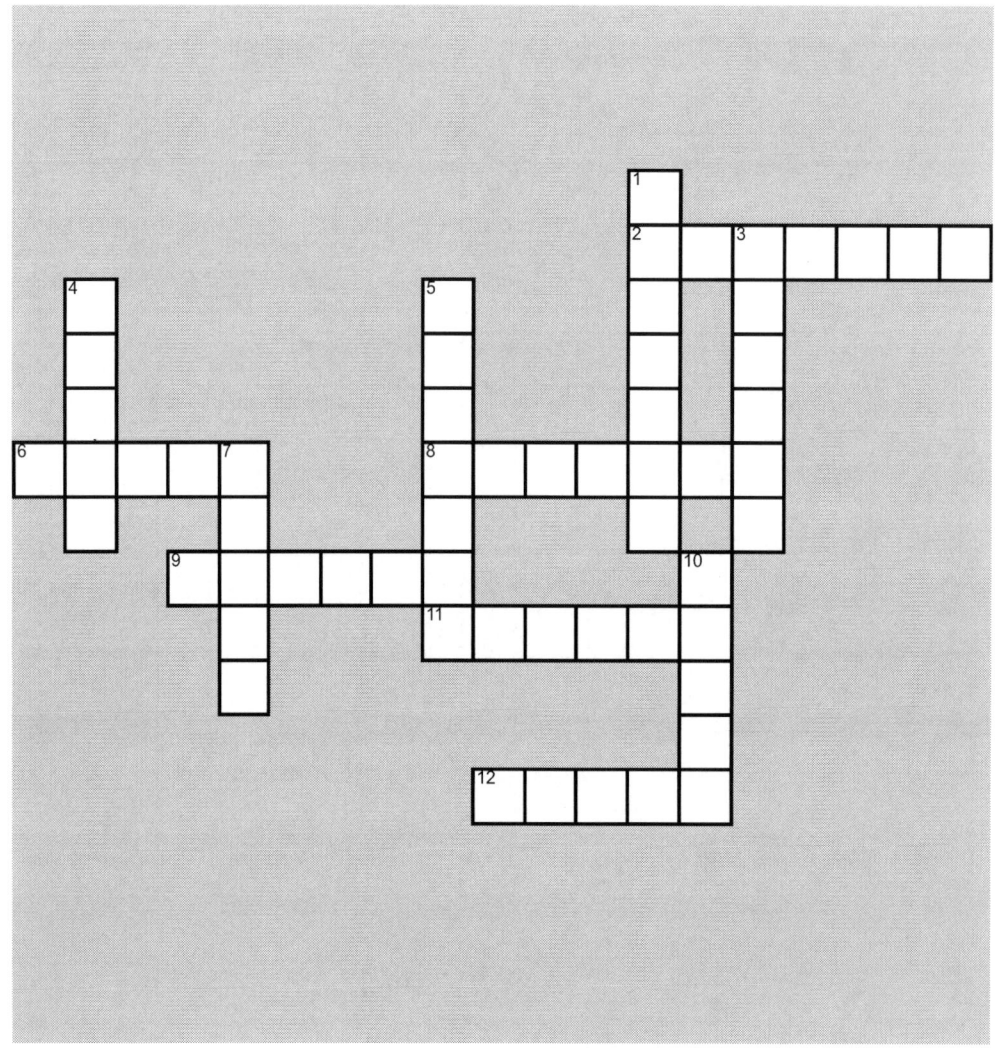

Across

2 noun - a mountainous region of central Italy on the Adriatic

6 noun - genus of tropical plants with creeping rootstocks and small umbellate flowers

8 salutation used in india by raising both hands in front of the face

9 noun - fruit-flavored dessert (trade mark Jell-O) made from a commercially prepared gelatin powder

11 noun - a port city on the Gulf of Finland that is the capital and largest city of Estonia

12 A shade of the color green

Down

1 A crystalline variety of fruit sugar obtained from dambonite.

3 verb - break into lumps before sorting; "rag ore"

4 adjective - of or relating to feces; "fecal matter"

5 Most fervent or sharp

7 the language spoken by the Aleut

10 To divest of the traits of a boy.

Crossword Puzzle

Across

2 noun - a genetic abnormality resulting in short stature

6 Yielding or trembling under the feet as moist or boggy ground; shaking; moving.

8 An armed constable; also a government servant or courier.

9 noun - an area in southwestern Asia whose sovereignty is disputed between Pakistan and India

11 verb - remove (water) from a vessel with a container

12 noun - a workman who laces shoes or footballs or books (during binding)

Down

1 verb - receive into the mind and retain; "Imbibe ethical principles"

3 adjective - (British informal) sore or lame; "a gammy foot"

4 adjective - relating to the blood vessels or blood

5 noun - a capacitance unit equal to one billion farads

7 verb - become imbued; "The liquids light and gases absorb"

10 noun - a South American plant that is cultivated for its large fragrant trumpet-shaped flowers

Crossword Puzzle

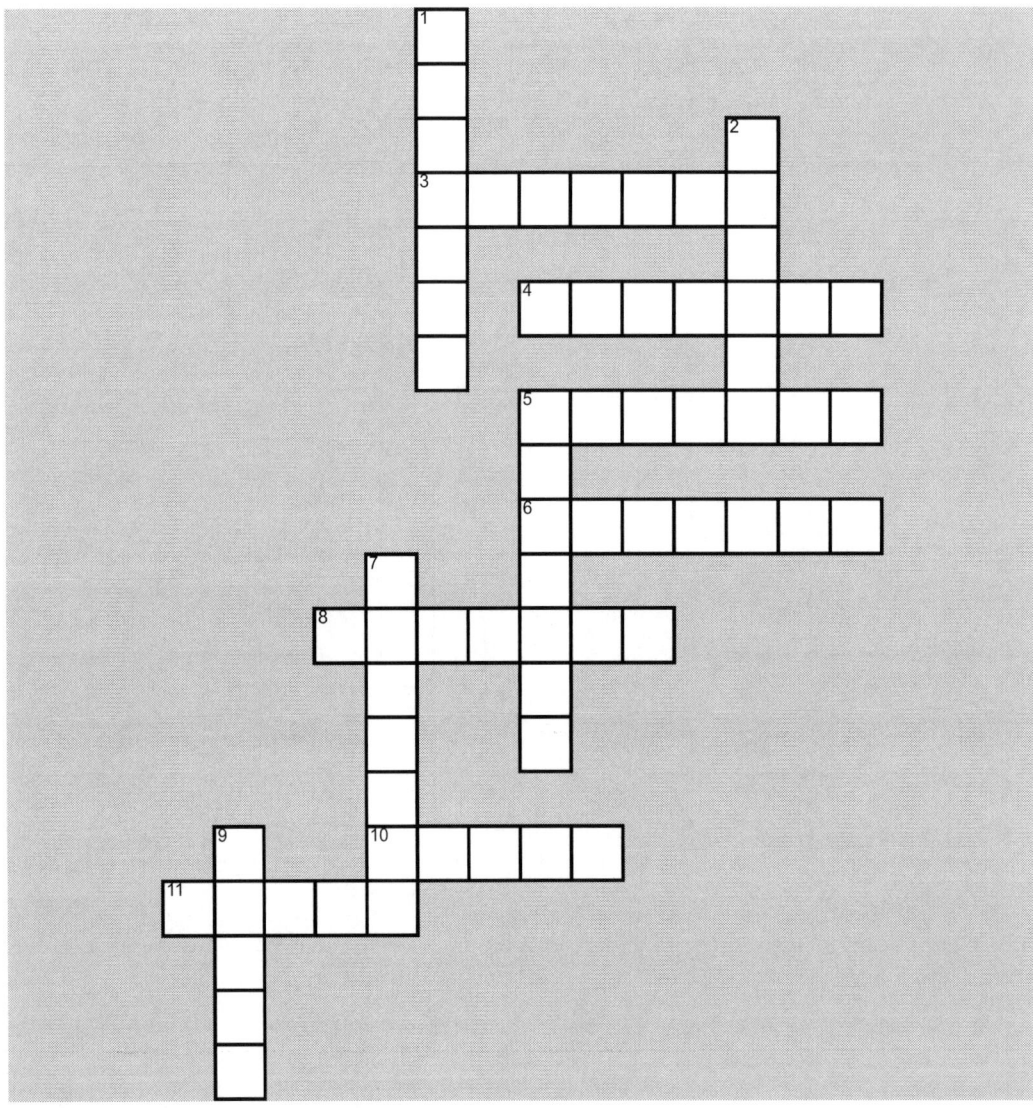

Across

3 An ancient area of Central Asia also home to the Bactrian Camel.

4 Compensation for the injury done by slaying a kinsman.

5 Woven like damask. -- n. A damass

6 apply (usually a liquid) to a surface; "dab the wall with paint"

8 verb - convert into lime; "the salts calcified the rock"

10 noun - a narrow thin strip of wood used as backing for plaster or to make latticework

11 noun - short underpants for women or children (usually used in the plural)

Down

1 Talk at incessantly

2 noun - a group of 21 volcanic islands in the North Atlantic between Iceland and the Shetland Islands

5 A follower of Dadaism art movement that flourished in Europe early in the 20th century

7 adverb - in a vague way; "he looked vaguely familiar"; "he explained it somewhat mistily"

9 informal British term for a cafe

Crossword Puzzle

Across

2 Jordan's port; located in southwestern Jordan on the Gulf of Aqaba

5 noun - inability to walk

7 verb - laugh at with contempt and derision; "The crowd jeered at the speaker"

11 noun - the quantity that a bag will hold; "he ate a large bag of popcorn"

12 The driver of a hack or carriage for public hire.

Down

1 noun - an overland journey by hunters (especially in Africa)

3 noun - a jar for holding jellies or preserves

4 A light skiff or rowboat used on the Bosporus; also a Levantine vessel of larger size.

6 noun - a distinctive fragrant flavor characteristic of vanilla beans

8 noun - mammal of South Africa that resembled a zebra; extinct since late 19th century

9 pertaining to the Greek philosopher Galen

10 noun - (ethnic slur) offensive term for Black people

Crossword Puzzle

Across

2 noun - United States writer of satirical novels (1879-1958)

4 noun - the larva of the housefly and blowfly commonly found in decaying organic matter

6 noun - genus of Old World herbs: dead nettles; henbits

9 noun - the French-speaking part of the Canadian Maritime Provinces

10 noun - people who are condemned to eternal punishment; "he felt he had visited the realm of the damned"

11 Liable to roll over; crank; as a walty ship.

12 noun - a person whose occupation is making and altering garments

Down

1 noun - Irish poet and dramatist (1865-1939)

3 A lazy or cowardly person; a rascal.

5 noun - the driver and keeper of an elephant

7 noun - (physics) a device that attracts iron and produces a magnetic field

8 noun - fortuneteller who predicts your future by the lines on your palms

Crossword Puzzle

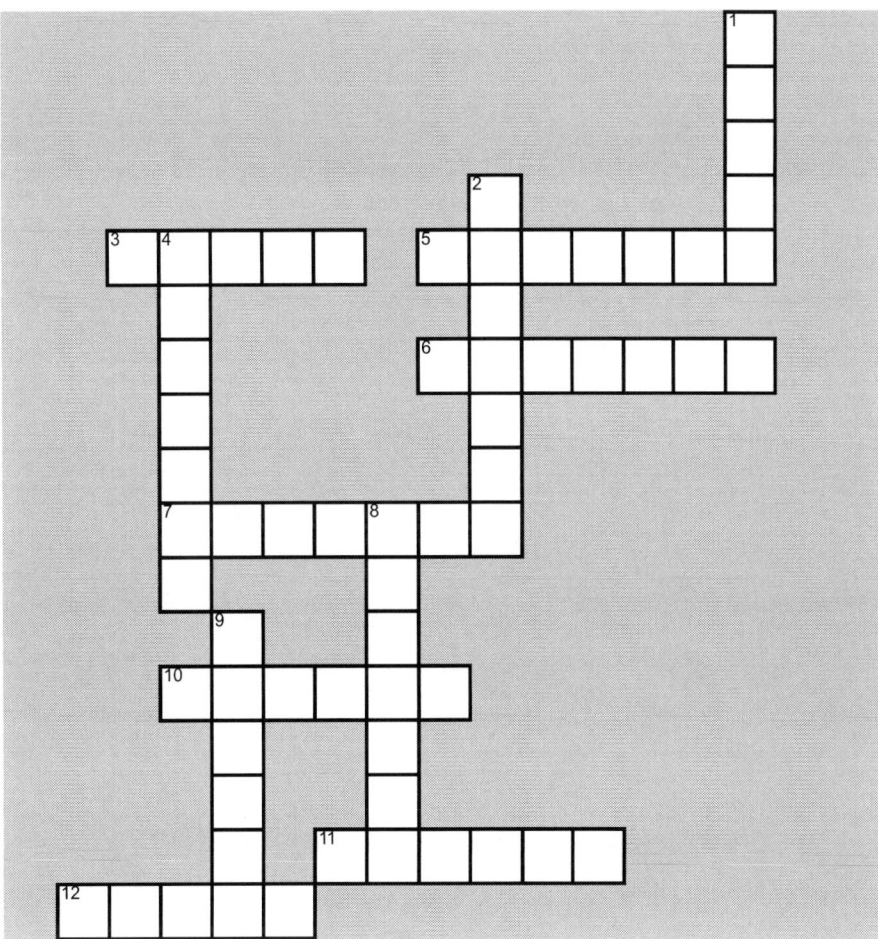

Across

3 County name of Shropshire 1974-80

5 noun - (classical antiquity) a crescent-shaped seagoing vessel propelled by oars

6 noun - the craniometric point at the junction of the anterior border of the lacrimal bone with the frontal bone

7 noun - United States liquid unit equal to 4 quarts or 3.785 liters

10 verb - search for something needed or desired; "Our babysitter raided our refrigerator"

11 noun - mouselike jumping rodent

12 noun - a person who awakes; "an early waker"

Down

1 a metal cleat on the bottom front of a horseshoe to prevent slipping

2 noun - genus of North American and east Asian perennial herbs; sometimes included in genus Prenanthes

4 To take away by judicial decision.

8 Sheathed; having an ocrea or ochrea which is a fusion of plant stipules forming a shield

9 verb - colour with streaks or blotches of different shades

Crossword Puzzle

Across

2 of leaves etc; growing in pairs on either side of a stem; "opposite leaves"

3 A thin leaf of metal as for use in gilding or enameling or to show through a translucent medium.

7 an idealized place of great or idyllic magnificence and beauty.

8 A round gall produced on the leaves and shoots of various species of the oak tree. See Gall and Nutgall.

10 noun - a light medieval helmet with a slit for vision

11 noun - the act of damaging something or someone

Down

1 noun - a sharply directional antenna

3 noun - tree native to southeastern Asia having reddish wood with a mottled or striped black grain

4 noun - a large waterfall on the border between Argentina and Brazil

5 stab or pierce; "he jabbed the piece of meat with his pocket knife"

6 noun - discriminatory or abusive behavior towards members of another race

9 noun - (Yiddish) a thief or dishonest person or scoundrel (often used as a general term of abuse)

Crossword Puzzle

Across

2 adjective - of or relating to a quantum or capable of existing in only one of two states

5 Giant Bulrush of New Zealand

6 a tortilla chip topped with cheese and chili-pepper and broiled

8 noun - dilatation or distension of a hollow organ

10 noun - rapacious seabird that pursues weaker birds to make them drop their prey

11 king of Northumbria who was converted to Christianity (585-633)

12 noun - a container for something to be mailed

Down

1 verb - influence or urge by gentle urging caressing or flattering; "He palavered her into going along"

3 noun - a coarse file with sharp pointed projections

4 verb - separate with a railing; "rail off the crowds from the Presidential palace"

7 adjective - existing in abundance; "abounding confidence"; "whiskey galore"

9 noun - an ancient city in northwestern Iran; known for hot springs

Crossword Puzzle

Across

2 noun - a body of water cut off from a larger body by a reef of sand or coral

4 verb - clean with a vacuum cleaner; "vacuum the carpets"

9 noun - a person who wagers money on the outcome of games or sporting events

10 1. One that greets acclaims or catches someone's attention. 2. A bullhorn.

11 verb - do away with; "Slavery was abolished in the mid-19th century in America and in Russia"

12 less well health deteriorating during a period of sickness

Down

1 noun - an industrial city in the European part of Russia

3 an organization of military vessels belonging to a country and available for sea warfare

5 verb - influence or urge by gentle urging caressing or flattering; "He palavered her into going along"

6 reveal the true nature of; "The journal article unmasked the corrupt politician"

7 A clay mineral that is a polymorph of kaolinite.

8 noun - the area for food preparation on a ship

Crossword Puzzle

Across

2 A card die. or domino having four spots or pips

3 An alloy (formerly) used to coat fuel rods in nuclear power stations.

5 noun - a computer program that attaches labels to the grammatical constituents of textual matter

7 noun - someone who rows a boat

10 a plot to carry out some harmful or illegal act (especially a political plot)

12 noun - small Arctic whale the male having a long spiral ivory tusk

Down

1 noun - an edible American clam; the heavy shells were used as money by some American Indians

4 noun - padding that is worn inside a brassiere

6 noun - a tributary of the Ohio River in West Virginia

8 noun - the iridescent internal layer of a mollusk shell

9 A close; a yard; a croft; a garden; as a cloister garth.

11 verb - emit long loud cries; "wail in self-pity"; "howl with sorrow"

Crossword Puzzle

Across

4 City founded by Sargon the Great of Mesopotamia.

6 verb - remove with or as if with a ladle; "ladle the water out of the bowl"

7 Glossy dark brown kelp with broad fronds

8 noun - medium-sized tree-dwelling monkey of the Amazon basin; only New World monkey with a short tail

11 noun - an esoteric or occult matter resembling the Kabbalah that is traditionally secret

Down

1 a person whose head is bald

2 A callous tumor on the leg of a horse below the hock.

3 The person to whom another is bound or the person to whom a bond is given.

5 noun - a winged sandal (as worn by Hermes in Graeco-Roman art)

8 verb - take away the weapons from; render harmless

9 noun - a pocket-size case for holding papers and paper money

10 noun - a ribbed woven fabric of silk or rayon or cotton

Crossword Puzzle

Across

1 Provencal beef and red wine stew
4 noun - a mountain lake (especially one formed by glaciers)
10 Donkey - Friend of Pooh Bear
11 noun - a paved surface having compressed layers of broken rocks held together with tar
12 noun - an owner or proprietor of an inn in Italy

Down

2 verb - remove (water) from a vessel with a container
3 Celebes megapode that lays eggs in holes in sandy beaches
5 Pertaining to the jejunum.
6 A kind of rubblework. In the United States any rubblework of thin and small stones.
7 noun - an attendant who carries the golf clubs for a player
8 noun - the first Hindu calendar month (corresponding to March in the Gregorian calendar)
9 a cause for feeling concern; "his major care was the illness of his wife"

Crossword Puzzle

Across

3 noun - shading consisting of multiple crossing lines

4 noun - a thin plate or layer (especially of bone or mineral)

5 noun - someone who jeers or mocks or treats something with contempt or calls out in derision

8 verb - measure (distances) by pacing; "step off ten yards"

9 To remove from condition of being a nun.

10 noun - any of numerous conifers of the genus Larix all having deciduous needlelike leaves

11 verb - talk profusely; "she was yakking away about her grandchildren"

Down

1 noun - a very wealthy or powerful businessman; "an oil baron"

2 Very great; huge; vast; also monstrous in character; inhuman; atrocious; fierce.

6 noun - a port city in southwestern Croatia on the Adriatic; a popular tourist center

7 Town in Tyne and Wear known for its march in the depression to Westminster

11 verb - look with amazement; look stupidly

Crossword Puzzle

Across

3 (Arabic) a loose black robe from head to toe; traditionally worn by Muslim women

4 an intricate traditional dance in India performed by professional dancing girls

6 noun - egg-shaped terra cotta wind instrument with a mouthpiece and finger holes

7 noun - a fence made of upright pickets

10 United States playwright (1906-1963)

11 British slang for denoting a loutish female or male.

12 People of Kerala formerly a military caste.

Down

1 noun - a small flag used by surveyors or soldiers to mark a position

2 a convenient package or parcel (as of cigarettes or film)

5 A salt of an octoic acid; a caprylate.

8 verb - take exception to; "She challenged his claims"

9 verb - disturb (someone's) composure; "The audience was jolted by the play"

Crossword Puzzle

Across

2 a farewell remark; "they said their good-byes"

3 adjective - deviating from a square or circle or sphere by being elongated in one direction

8 noun - a civil or military authority in Turkey or Egypt

10 noun - a wheeled vehicle adapted to the rails of railroad; "three cars had jumped the rails"

11 noun - the state or quality of being widely honored and acclaimed

12 noun - well-seasoned stew of meat and vegetables

Down

1 noun - the 7th letter of the Hebrew alphabet

4 viscera and trimmings of a butchered animal often considered inedible by humans

5 noun - any shape that is triangular in cross section

6 noun - West Indian tree yielding a hard dark brown wood resembling mahogany in texture and value

7 a popular vacation spot in the Canadian Rockies

9 An earthwork; a mound; a raised work.

Crossword Puzzle

Across

1 A public shed or portico for travelers worshipers etc.

4 verb - shift to a counterclockwise direction; "the wind backed"

5 A Russian measure of length equal to about seven English feet.

7 noun - the language of the Tagalog on which Filipino is based

8 Of or pertaining to the Cabiri or to their mystical worship.

11 superlative of tame. most tame.

Down

2 adjective - suggestive of youth; vigorous and fresh; "he is young for his age"

3 grassy strip by the sea

5 noun - a stout sword with a curved blade and thick back

6 noun - small genus of evergreen tropical shrubs or trees with smooth leathery leaves

9 noun - an Eskimo hut; usually built of blocks (of sod or snow) in the shape of a dome

10 noun - steps consisting of two parallel members connected by rungs; for climbing up or down

Crossword Puzzle

Across

2. noun - a port on Alaska's southern coast from which oil is shipped to markets around the world
5. A drinking vessel. See Quaich.
6. noun - (ethnic slur) offensive term for Black people
9. noun - a long depression in the surface of the land that usually contains a river
10. the enclosed compartment of an aircraft or spacecraft where passengers are carried
11. adverb - in a natty manner; with smartness; "it was arranged carefully and nattily"

Down

1. stuffed filled with stuffing
3. The state of needing or of suffering a natural want.
4. an almost pleasurable sensation of fright; "a frisson of surprise shot through him"
6. noun - god of agriculture and the earth; national god of Philistines
7. noun - small New Zealand broadleaf evergreen tree often cultivated in warm regions as an ornamental
8. characteristic of male adolescents or young men being rowdymacho or immature

Crossword Puzzle

Across

2 back and sides of a hog salted and dried or smoked; usually sliced thin and fried

4 noun - the Iranian language of the Zoroastrian literature of the 3rd to 10th centuries

7 noun - large family of important mostly marine food fishes

9 lift with a special device; "jack up the car so you can change the tire"

11 One who steals and drives away cattle or beasts by herds or droves.

12 noun - a soft wet area of low-lying land that sinks underfoot

Down

1 noun - a port city in northeastern Tanzania on the Indian Ocean

3 noun - French politician who proposed the Maginot Line (1877-1932)

5 noun - a Chadic language spoken south of Lake Chad

6 A long pole on two wheels used in hauling logs.

8 adverb - alongside each other facing in the same direction

10 noun - back part of the head or skull

Crossword Puzzle

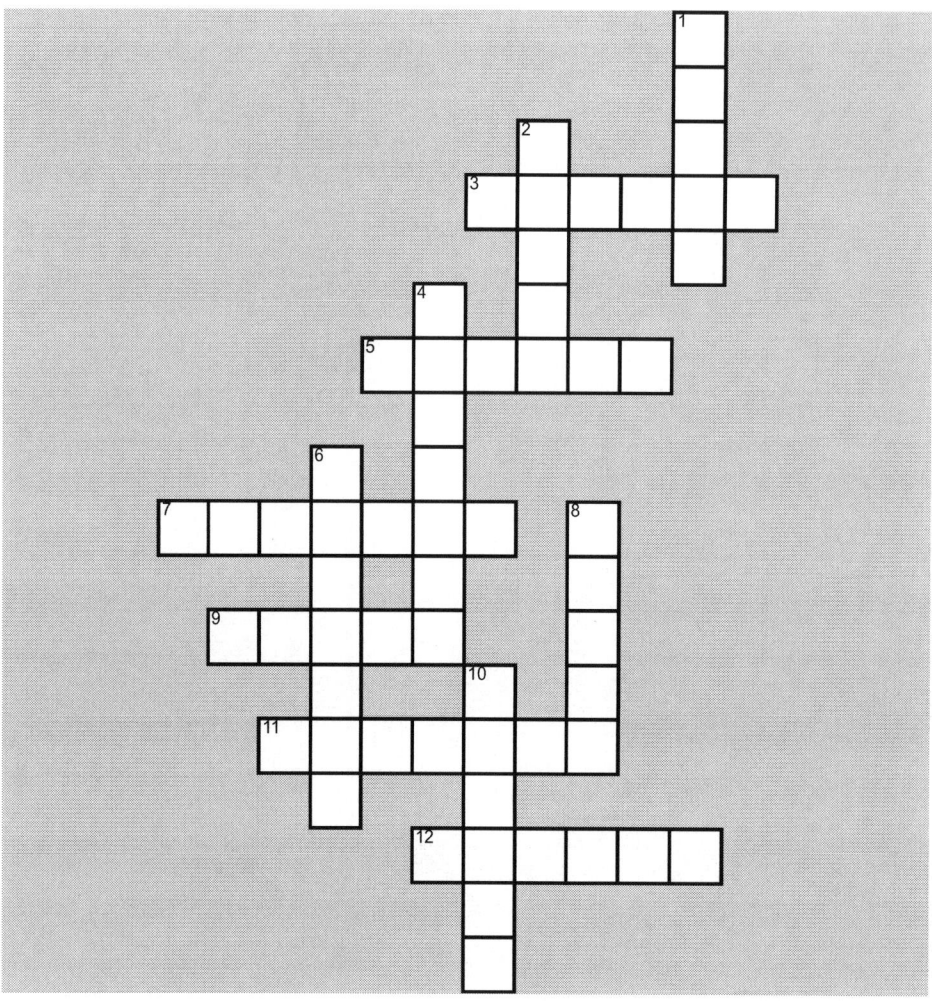

Across

3 noun - worthless or oversimplified ideas

5 1. A type of milk curd cheese used in Indian Iranian and Afghan cooking.

7 noun - small genus of perennial herbs or subshrubs; some often placed in other genera

9 Uglis: a kind of tangelo. A cross between a tangerine a grapefruit and an orange.

11 noun - unrefined brown sugar made from palm sap

12 adjective - muted or unclear; "veiled sounds"; "the image is veiled or foggy"

Down

1 used as a Hindi courtesy title; equivalent to English `Mr'

2 noun - a story about mythical or supernatural beings or events

4 noun - type genus of the family Balanidae

6 noun - a line of track providing a runway for wheels; "he walked along the railroad track"

8 needy people collectively; "they try to help the needy"

10 Lying at length; as the jacent posture.

Crossword Puzzle

Across

2 Pertaining to ulmin; designating an acid obtained from ulmin.

5 noun - a socially awkward or tactless act

7 wild ox of mountainous areas of eastern India

9 noun - an insignia used by the medical profession; modeled after the staff of Hermes

10 verb - make into a bale; "bale hay"

11 noun - a musical composition written for eight performers

Down

1 noun - the inner and longer of the two bones of the human forearm

3 noun - long-winged web-footed aquatic bird of the gull family

4 verb - make moist; "The dew moistened the meadows"

6 noun - a body of (usually fresh) water surrounded by land

8 noun - shrubby plant with aromatic greyish-green leaves used as a cooking herb

9 noun - an attendant who carries the golf clubs for a player

Crossword Puzzle

Across

3 To awake; to arouse; to stir or start up; also to shout out.

5 noun - tawny brown North American thrush noted for its song

8 noun - alternatively a member of the family Nymphaeaceae; a small genus of American aquatic plants

10 verb - make a trip for pleasure

11 noun - worship of Shakti as the wife of Shiva

12 Consisting of rays as light.

Down

1 adjective the comparative form of safe less likely to be harmful

2 To revoke as a legacy grant etc. or to satisfy it by some other gift.

4 verb - choose not to consume; "I abstain from alcohol"

6 noun - a rectangular groove made to hold two pieces together

7 noun - dilatation or distension of a hollow organ

9 adjective - free from artificiality; "a lifelike pose"; "a natural reaction"

Crossword Puzzle

Across

2 a fee charged for exchanging currencies

5 Of or pertaining to Eden; paradisaic.

7 verb - make walk; "He walks the horse up the mountain"; "Walk the dog twice a day"

8 noun - a quality proceeding from feelings of affection or love

9 noun - any garden plant of the genus Alyssum having clusters of small yellow or white flowers

12 verb - draw the cork from (bottles); "uncork the French wine"

Down

1 verb - pull or move with a sudden movement; "He turned the handle and jerked the door open"

3 Meaning stranger. eg. The cat was odder than the other one.

4 noun - the termination of someone's employment (leaving them free to depart)

6 noun - New World lizards

10 adjective - adapted to wandering or roaming

11 noun - organized crime in Japan; an alliance of criminal organizations and illegal enterprises

Crossword Puzzle

Across

3 Dimness or obscurity of sight dependent upon a speck on the cornea; also the speck itself.

4 noun - a laborer who is obliged to do menial work

7 noun - small Asiatic wild bird; believed to be ancestral to domestic fowl

10 noun - an overwhelming feeling of fear and anxiety

11 Genus of trees or shrubs with coriaceous leaves typified by the holly

12 noun - in former times was free and cultivated his own land

Down

1 Past tense/past participle of 'abide'.

2 noun - island country in the Atlantic to the east of Florida and Cuba; a popular winter resort

5 verb - make lighter or brighter; "This lamp lightens the room a bit"

6 noun - small wooden bat with a flat surface; used for hitting balls in various games

8 noun - the brother of your father or mother; the husband of your aunt

9 verb - be opposite; "the facing page"; "the two sofas face each other"

Crossword Puzzle

Across

2 A hypothetical particle that always moves faster than light

5 adjective - (used especially of clothes) marked by conspicuous display

6 verb - go back to bad behavior; "Those who recidivate are often minor criminals"

7 The son of Amminadab in the book of Numbers.

9 Irish or scottish for fool.

11 verb - speak (about unimportant matters) rapidly and incessantly

12 noun - a racketeer assigned to collect or distribute payoff money

Down

1 a Latin American dance similar in rhythm to the rumba

3 verb - have affection for; feel tenderness for

4 A small piece of money in value about a farthing or a half cent.

8 One of an important religious sect in India which regards Siva with peculiar veneration.

10 noun - the amount that a container (as a wine bottle or tank) lacks of being full

Crossword Puzzle

Across

3 noun - anthropologist and linguist; studied languages of North American Indians (1884-1939)

4 noun - a Russian unit of length (1.067 km)

7 noun - the act of pausing uncertainly; "there was a hesitation in his speech"

11 noun - a town in southwestern British Columbia on Vancouver Island to the west of Vancouver

12 noun - cubes of meat marinated and cooked on a skewer usually with vegetables

Down

1 noun - a unit of resistance equal to a billionth of an ohm

2 noun - a visible suspension in the air of particles of some substance

5 noun - the act of consuming food

6 noun - pen where racehorses are saddled and paraded before a race

8 noun - a communication system based on broadcasting electromagnetic waves

9 To untwist; as to unlay a rope.

10 Pertaining to zinc or having its appearance.

Crossword Puzzle

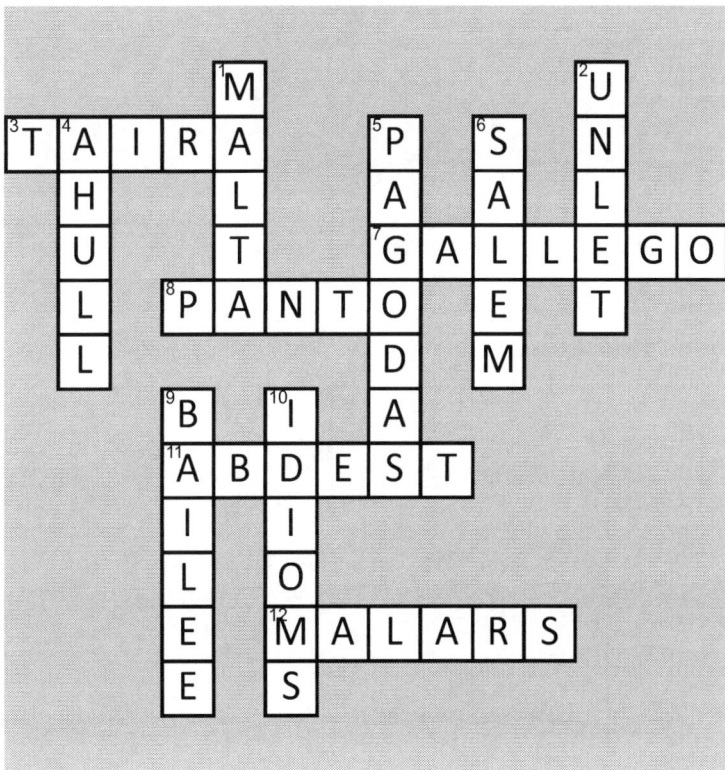

Across

3 noun - long-tailed arboreal mustelid of Central America and South America

7 A native or inhabitant of Galicia in Spain; a Galician.

8 noun - an abbreviation of pantomime

11 Purification by washing the hands before prayer; -- a Muslim rite.

12 noun - the arch of bone beneath the eye that forms the prominence of the cheek

Down

1 a strategically located island to the south of Sicily in the Mediterranean Sea

2 Of a property - not let or rented out.

4 With the sails furled and the helm lashed alee; -- applied to ships in a storm. See Hull n.

5 noun - an Asian temple; usually a pyramidal tower with an upward curving roof

6 noun - a city in southern India

9 noun - the agent to whom property involved in a bailment is delivered

10 noun - the style of a particular artist or school or movement; "an imaginative orchestral idiom"

Crossword Puzzle

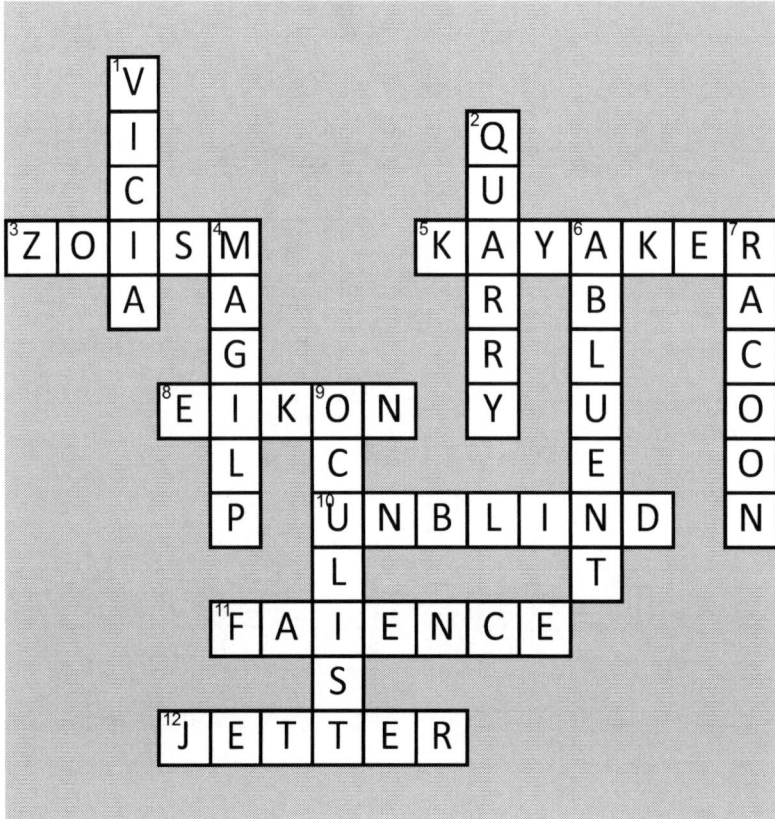

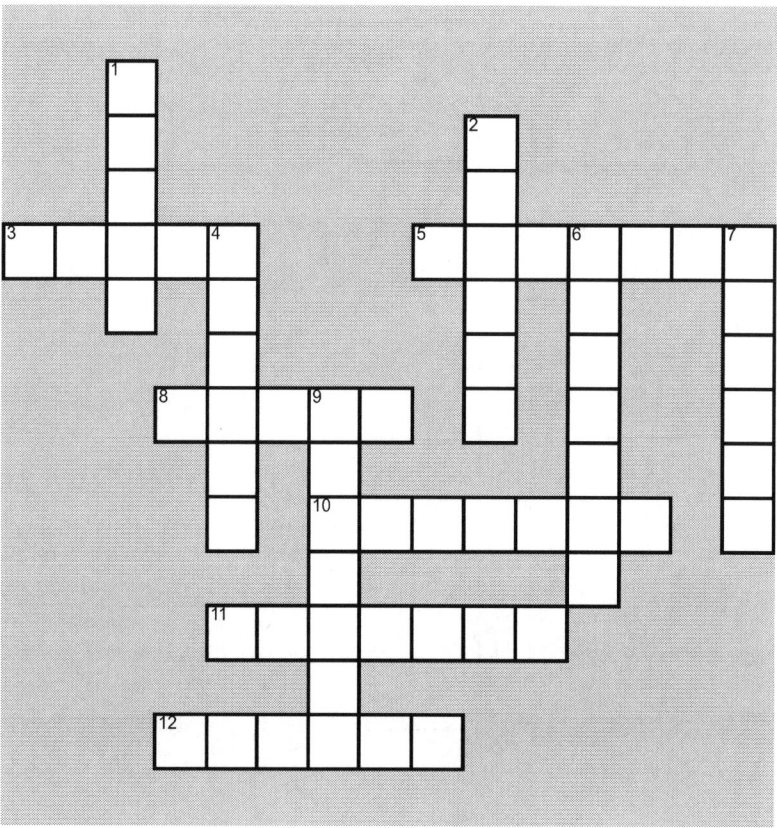

Across

3 Reverence for animal life or belief in animal powers and influences as among savages.

5 One who uses a kayak.

8 An image or effigy; -- used rather in an abstract sense and rarely for a work of art.

10 To free from blindness; to give or restore sight to; to open the eyes of.

11 noun - glazed earthenware decorated with opaque colors

12 One who struts; one who bears himself jauntily; a fop.

Down

1 noun - widely distributed genus of annual or perennial and often climbing herbs

2 verb - extract (something such as stones) from or as if from a quarry; "quarry marble"

4 noun - a medium for oil-paints; linseed oil mixed with mastic varnish or turpentine

6 Washing away; carrying off impurities; detergent. -- n. (Med.) A detergent.

7 noun - an omnivorous nocturnal mammal native to North America and Central America

9 noun - a medical doctor specializing in the diagnosis and treatment of diseases of the eye

Crossword Puzzle

Across

2 lift with a special device; "jack up the car so you can change the tire"

3 verb - place in a cylindrical vessel; "jar the jam"

5 noun - a young unmarried woman

7 adjective - of or relating to feces; "fecal matter"

8 a city in southern Turkey on the Seyhan River

9 noun - elegant sitting room where guests are received

11 noun - expandable metal or wooden wedge used by printers to lock up a form within a chase

Down

1 noun - any isomeric saturated hydrocarbon found in petroleum and used as a fuel and solvent

4 noun - a hiker who wears a backpack

6 craters formed by a volcanic eruption with little or none lava

7 hot spring therupeutic mud from Battaglio Italy

10 noun - Celtic god of love and beauty; patron deity of young men and women

Crossword Puzzle

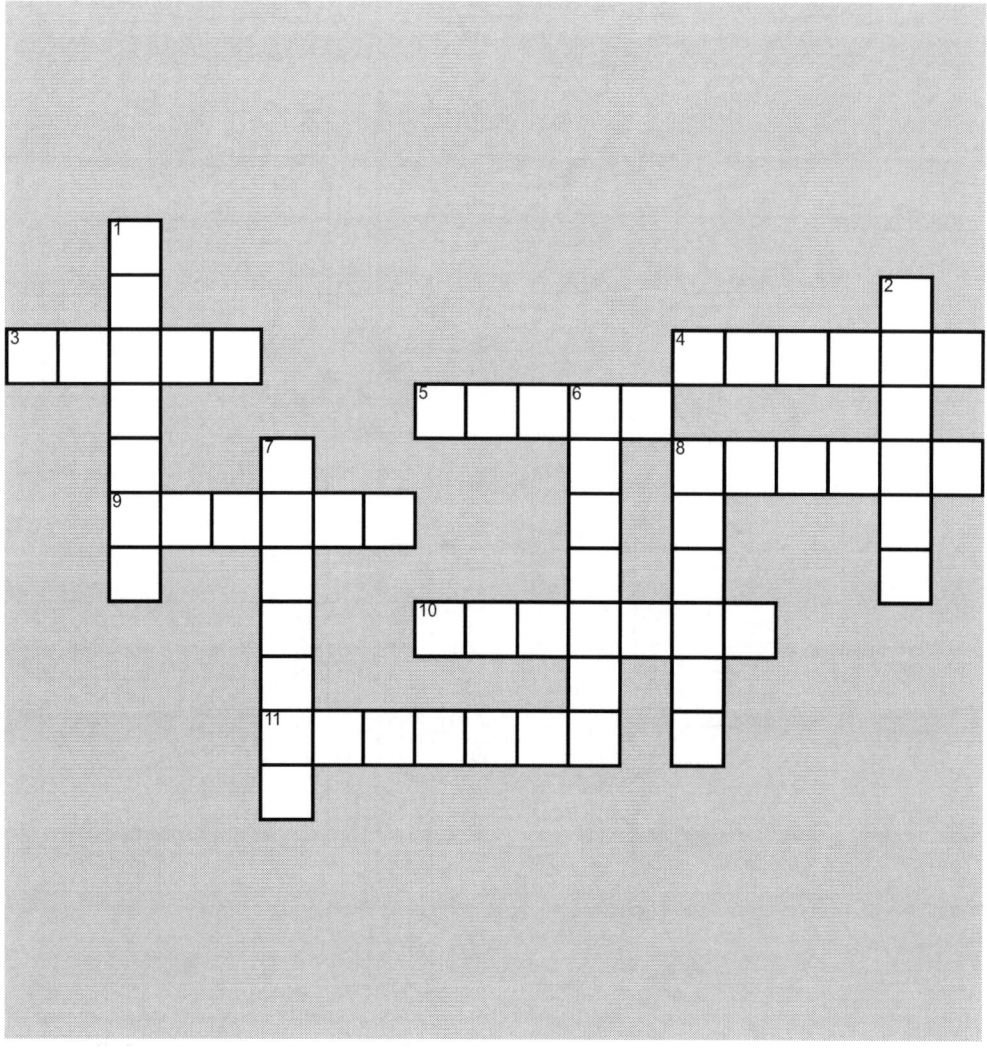

Across

3 verb - feed into; supply; "Her success feeds her vanity"

4 middle eastern or indian sweetmeat made of honey sesame seed rosewater saffron

5 noun - a Chadic language spoken south of Lake Chad

8 noun - an expensive vessel propelled by sail or power and used for cruising or racing

9 To take from or set free from a cart; to unload.

10 noun - a member of the Algonquian people of Maine and southern Quebec

11 noun - a bag in which rags are kept

Down

1 noun - the language of the Quechua which was spoken by the Incas

2 noun - a person who wants or needs something; "an owner of many things and needer of none"

6 noun - having no employment

7 noun - unrefined brown sugar made from palm sap

8 noun - an American (especially to non-Americans)

Crossword Puzzle

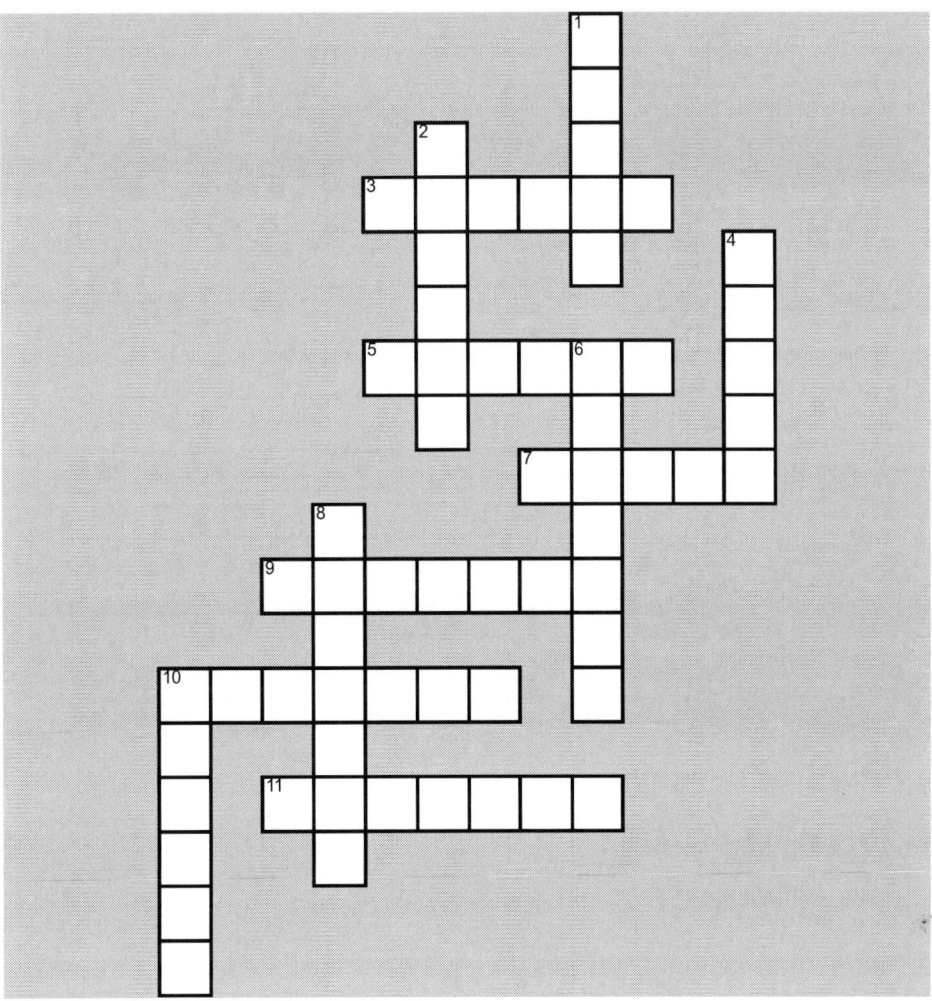

Across

3 verb - make warm or warmer; "The blanket will warm you"

5 noun - a burden (figuratively in the form of a bundle)

7 having a full range of physical or mental abilities; not disabled

9 noun - an omnivorous nocturnal mammal native to North America and Central America

10 noun - short-tailed monkey of rocky regions of Asia and Africa

11 noun - a homogeneous polynomial having at least two variables

Down

1 verb - set waves in; "she asked the hairdresser to wave her hair"

2 noun - the advisory board of the Tibetan government-in-exile

4 verb - look at with amorous intentions

6 noun - a gradual decline (in size or strength or power or number)

8 noun - type and sole extant genus of the Varanidae

10 noun - similar to McIntosh; juicy and late-ripening

Crossword Puzzle

Across

3 con man who tries to deceive members of the public

4 verb - act in a funny or teasing way

8 noun - a person with a prejudiced belief that one race is superior to others

9 noun - the tide while water is flowing out

10 adjective - still legally acceptable; "the license is still valid"

11 the trait of being rude and impertinent; inclined to take liberties

Down

1 verb - get stuck and immobilized; "the mechanism jammed"

2 Plant of the marigold family with bright orange or yellow flowers

5 noun - a variety of leafhopper

6 verb - cry weakly or softly; "she wailed with pain"

7 Sycophant; a person who praises powerful people in order to get their approval

8 noun - (the feminine of raja) a Hindu princess or the wife of a raja

Crossword Puzzle

Across

2 noun - someone who asks a question
4 noun - English rock star (born in 1943)
6 The military cloak of the Roman soldiers.
9 noun - proboscis monkeys
11 noun - Botswanan statesman who was the first president of Botswana (1921-1980)
12 An African carnivore (Nandinia binotata) allied to the civets. It is spotted with black.

Down

1 adjective - unequivocally detestable;
3 noun - a garment (coat or sweater) that has raglan sleeves
5 noun - the quality of threatening evil
7 noun - a recurrent rhythmical series
8 a unit of current equal to 10 amperes
10 noun - walking with your feet in shallow water

ANSWER

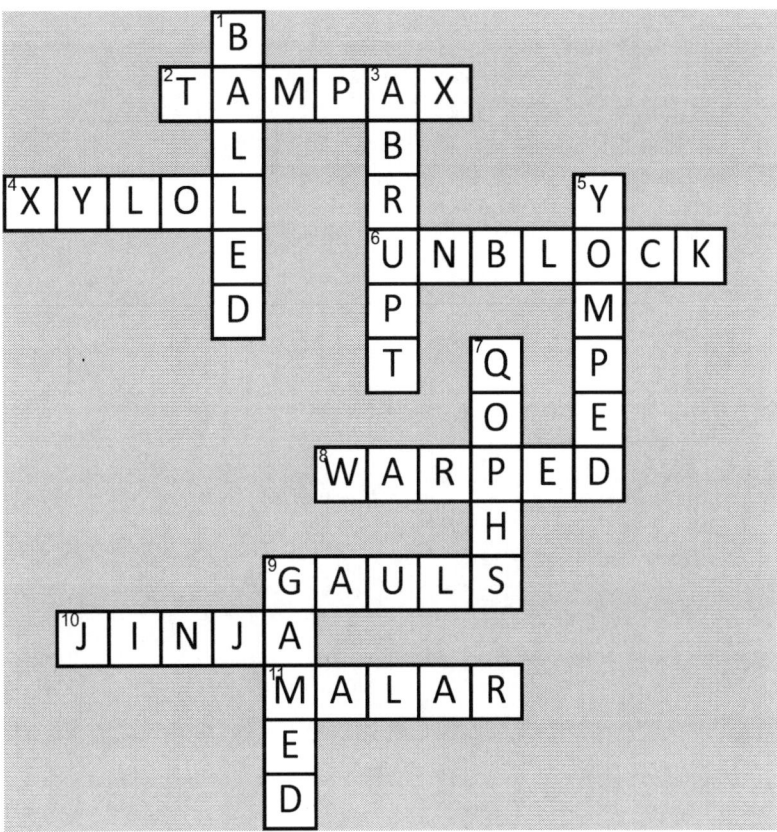

Made in the USA
Middletown, DE
12 June 2020